A BOOT UP

THE NORFOLK COAST

BOOK ONE

Tony Rothe

First published in Great Britain in 2009

Front cover: *View west from Skelding Hill*

British Library Cataloguing-in-Publication Data
A CIP record for this title is available from the British Library

ISBN 978 1 906887 01 8

PiXZ Books
Halsgrove House, Ryelands Industrial Estate,
Bagley Road, Wellington, Somerset TA21 9PZ
Tel: 01823 653777
Fax: 01823 216796
email: sales@halsgrove.com

An imprint of Halstar Ltd, part of the Halsgrove group of companies
Information on all Halsgrove ttles is available at: www.halsgrove.com

Printed and bound by D'Auria Industrie Grafiche, Italy

Contents

Introduction

The Norfolk coastline must be one of the most varied in Great Britain, including wild desolate fenlands, thriving docks and ports, towering cliffs, gently rolling countryside, isolated salt marshes, nationally famous bird reserves, shingle beaches, deserted sands, dramatic heathlands, a steam railway, and charming seaside towns and villages – it's all here for the discerning tourist. The area between Blakeney and Overstrand is one of the few areas of Norfolk that isn't flat – the last ice age just clipped the North Norfolk coast, and the glacier stopped a mile or two inland.

Therefore this stretch of coast is built mainly of moraine, ie debris left by the melting glacier when the ice age finished some 12000 years ago, and has been continually moulded and shaped by the weather and sea ever since.

This little book contains 12 walks covering the length of coast from Castle Rising, just north of the port of Kings Lynn, to Overstrand, just to the east of Cromer. There is something for everyone – Seaside, cliffs, fields, hills, marshes and heath, containing many wildlife habitats – walks that will appeal to every member of the family.

How to use this book

This book is not aimed at long distance walkers. You won't necessarily need long woolly socks, plus-fours, heavy rucksacks, or even proper walking boots, although waterproof footwear is recommended for some of the walks, especially in winter, or in wet weather.

All the walks are circular, ie they bring you back to your starting point, and are between 0.8 and 3.5 miles long, although some of the longer walks have optional short-cuts. When walking casually you will be doing about 2 miles per hour, a more purposeful pace will get you along at about 3 miles per hour, so the shortest walks need take you no more than half an hour, whereas the longest can take you up to two hours.

And it's difficult to get lost — whenever you get a glimpse of the sea, well that's always to the north. If it's midday, then the sun is to the south (more to the east in the morning, more to the west in the evening, but never due north !). However, carrying a compass is always a good idea.

Sketch maps are included, but if you want a definitive map, then the Ordnance Survey Explorer maps (1:25000 series) are unbeatable. The first 2 walks are on map 250 Norfolk Coast West, walks 3 to 7 are on map 251 Norfolk Coast Central, whereas the rest are on map 252 Norfolk Coast East.

Starting points are given, together with the British Grid reference which will enable you to find the spot on any Ordnance Survey map. Each starting point provides somewhere to park, but in some cases there may be a parking fee. A regular bus service, known as the "Coasthopper" (www.norfolkgreen.co.uk) runs along the coast linking many of the walks; walk 8 is served by the excellent "Poppy Line" steam railway; and Cromer, Sheringham, and West Runton are on the Bittern Line railway route. Nearest toilets and refreshments are suggested, but you must realise that many places are seasonal, so please don't complain if the ice cream man isn't where you expect to find him on a bitterly cold Tuesday morning in February!

The difficulty of each walk is indicated by a "boot" rating, based mainly on the quality of the paths, the gradients, and likely amount of mud! However, these are based on Norfolk standards: Compared to many walks in the Lake District or Pennines, the walks in this book would probably all rank as "1 boot". Most of these walks are not suitable for push-chairs, but this information is also given for each walk.

So, please use this little book to explore a very beautiful corner of a wonderful and varied part of the UK, and have fun doing so.

Tony Rothe, December 2008

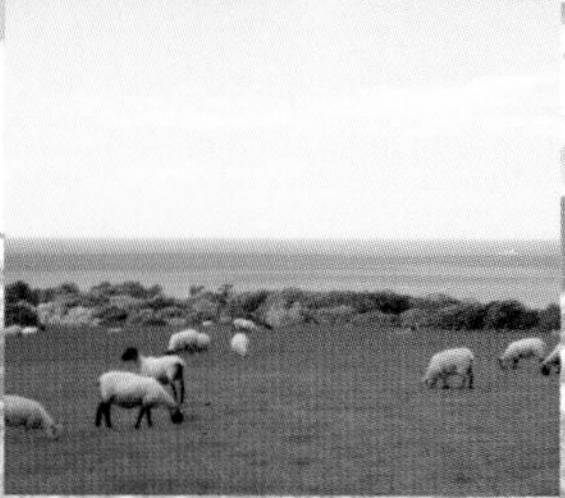

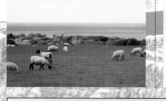

Key to Symbols Used

Level of difficulty:

Easy (one symbol)

Moderate (two symbols)

More challenging (three symbols)

Map symbols:

- Park & start
- Tarred Road
- Unpaved road
- Footpath
- Building
- Church
- Triangulation pillar or other landmark
- WC
- Refreshments
- Pub

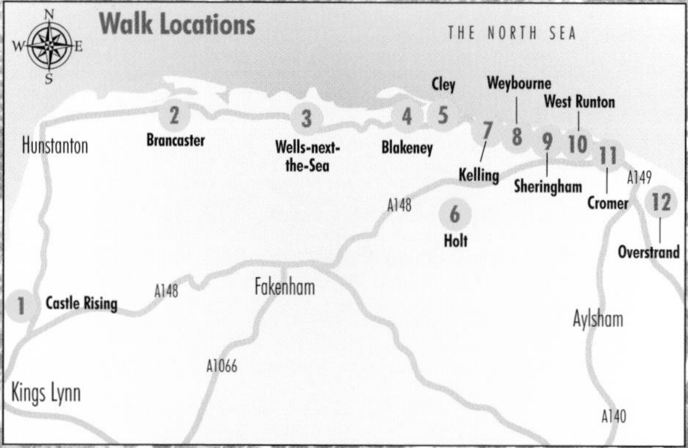
Walk Locations
N
W
E
S
THE NORTH SEA
1 Castle Rising
2 Brancaster
3 Wells-next-the-Sea
4 Blakeney
5 Cley
6 Holt
7 Kelling
8 Weybourne
9 Sheringham
10 West Runton
11 Cromer
12 Overstrand
Hunstanton
Fakenham
Aylsham
Kings Lynn
A148
A148
A149
A1066
A140

1 Castle Rising

Castle and Village: Meadows, fields, and a medieval castle

Night Marsh

Babingley Bridge

Babingley River

Castle Rising Wood

A149

Trinity Hospital

Castle

Castle Rising Village

WC

1 km
approximate scale

To Kings Lynn

The village of Castle Rising was once a thriving seaport, and pictures from the 18th century show that the Castle was still accessible by sea. The line of the coast must have changed radically during the following century, as the 19th Century railway line from Kings Lynn to Hunstanton passed to the west of the village, and the village is now some 4 miles from the sea. This pretty settlement is named after the nationally important Norman castle which towers over it.

Start/Parking: Castle Car Park: Free – English Heritage. (Open 10am to 6pm daily from 1st April to 1st November, 10am to 4pm, Wednesday to Sunday during the winter. Otherwise, parking in the village will be limited)

Map Ref: TF 667245
Nearest postcode PE31 6AH

Distance: 2.4 miles

Refreshments: Black Horse Public House, or Cafe in village

Toilets: In Car Park

Terrain: Fairly flat – good paths.

Transport: Coasthopper bus

Pushchairs: Yes

Difficulty:

Castle from the east

① Return to the road from the car park, then turn left to head north along the road towards the village and go straight over the cross-roads to continue heading north.

② Just before the last cottage on the right turn right into a pub-lic footpath beside that cottage. The sign for the footpath may be hidden by foliage and can easily be missed. The path is narrow at first, but soon becomes a broad grassy path, heading east along the left edge of a field, then north east along the edge of another field towards the main road. You will enjoy pleasant views to the north, and you have covered half a mile.

③ Turn left just before reaching the A149 Kings Lynn to Hunstanton road, to follow the path heading north alongside a grassy bank about 10m to the left of the road, but parallel to it. Unfortunately you will hear some noise from the traffic, but you will enjoy a walk surrounded by a wealth of wild flowers, such as clover, vetch, buttercups, campions, thistles, and soft rush.

④ Continue following the path north, and you will soon be beside a small river, called Babingley River, with occasional willows, and if it is summer, maybe dragonflies and peacock butterflies.

Cottages near the castle

Babingley River

The village of Castle Rising was once a thriving seaport, and pictures from the 18th century show that the Castle was still accessible by sea.

Streetlamp

5 After about a mile from the start of the walk, you will reach a small bridge, known as Babingley Bridge. Here you turn left to head south-west along a surfaced track, but you are unlikely to see any traffic, as the eastern end of this road is a dead end, and no longer accesses the A149. You may be lucky enough to spot a red deer in the field to your left as you approach Castle Rising wood. Continue along the road, now heading west, as you pass the wood. You have walked about a mile and a half.

6 When the road bends to the left, you should drop down to the right to take the grassy path which continues heading west, along the left edge of a field. The area to your right

Trinity Hospital

Castle Rising Castle has served as a hunting lodge, royal residence, and was home to the mother of Edward III, Queen Isabella, following her part in the murder of her husband Edward II. According to legend her screams are said to ring out over the village on nights of the full moon.

is known as the Night Marsh, and beyond it, in the parish of Babingley, the ruined ivy-covered tower of St Felix's church can still be seen.

7 When you reach a sign saying "Private – Conservation Area", turn left along the track

between the trees, to head south towards the village. Go through a 5-bar gate, and continue heading south, past some cottages, and at the end turn left to follow a path heading east beside a long wall. You will go past 2 cattle grids (but for safety please use the gates beside them),

and then go through a kissing gate onto the road.

8 Turn right to travel south again past the old Trinity Hospital, or Bede House, on your left, which was founded by the Earl of Northampton in 1614 as an

Road with no cars

St Felix Church

almshouse for elderly ladies. Turn right at the junction to continue heading south, past the Black Horse pub and follow the road as it bends to the right past the cafe. Turn left to continue south towards the castle.

9 When the road bends to the left, turn right into the castle grounds (when it is open). Follow the path past the castle, to emerge at the

end into the car park. Castle Rising Castle is one of the most famous 12th Century castles in England, with it's fine stone keep, built around AD1140, and massive surrounding earthworks. Rising has served as a hunting lodge, royal residence, and was home to the mother of Edward III, Queen Isabella, following her part in the murder of her husband Edward II. According to legend her screams are said to ring out

over the village on nights of the full moon. The castle passed to the Howard family in 1544 and is currently owned by Lord Howard of Rising, a descendant of William D'Albini II, the Norman baron who built the castle. The property is managed by English Heritage and is well worth a visit before you return to your car. Tickets are available from the small building you will pass on your path.

2 **Brancaster**

Barrow Common and Coast Path: Heath, fields, and a Roman fort

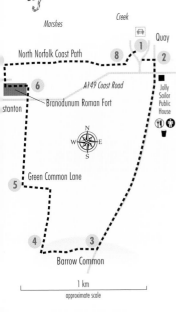

Marshes

Creek

Quay

North Norfolk Coast Path

①

⑧

②

A149 Coast Road

⑥

Branodunum Roman Fort

stanton

Jolly
Sailor
Public
House

N
W·(+)·E
S

Green Common Lane

⑤

④

③

Barrow Common

1 km
approximate scale

Brancaster's main claim to fame is the Roman fort, the site of which lies between the villages of Brancaster and Brancaster Staithe. Not much is known about the fort, except that it was known as "Branodunum", and located at the area now known as Rack Hill. Being quite remote, it would have been a minor outpost, built in the second century AD, and established to guard against attack by sea. The walk also includes the beautiful Barrow Common. Dial House, on the staithe itself, is a National Trust Millennium Activity Centre, which offers residential and day courses for families,

Start/Parking: Brancaster Staithe – Free – just West of Burnham Deepdale, on the staithe itself.
Map ref: TF 792444
Nearest postcode PE31 8BW
Distance: 2.8 miles
Refreshments: Jolly Sailors pub; or the refreshment hut on the staithe.
Toilets: Jolly Sailors pub (for customers).
Terrain: Country lanes, grassy paths, meadows and a boardwalk across a marsh.
Transport: Coasthopper bus
Pushchairs: NO (several kissing gates and a narrow boardwalk)
Difficulty: 🥾 🥾

adults and school groups, including kayaking, sailing, orienteering, and ecology awareness.

The Quay

① From the car park on the staithe, start to head south back towards the main road, but turn left along a footpath beside a fence, signposted as the Coast Path, which takes you past the newly rebuilt fishing quay. The original quay was built in 1750, but gradually deteriorated so as to become virtually unusable to all but the smallest craft. The new quay, costing over a quarter of a million pounds, was opened in 2007 to boost the local fishing industry, and enable the local fishermen to meet the demand for the high quality local fish.

② At the quay, turn right along a stony track to the main coast road. Cross the road here, close to the Jolly Sailors pub, and continue south along the surfaced lane opposite. Continue along this road for about half a mile, gently climbing, until you reach the start of Barrow Common. The prolific and pungent wild flower growing beside this road in spring and early summer is Alexander, introduced to Britain as a delicacy by the Romans, but confined to the coastal strip. By all means pause at the seat at the top of the road to enjoy the views before continuing. You will have travelled about 0.75 miles.

The Jolly Sailors

Barrow Common

3 Carry on south for a few more yards, then turn right onto the common, following a grassy path through the gorse, and heading broadly west. Barrow Common dates from at least the mid 18th century, and was requisitioned for military use during the Second World War (some of the buildings remain). It was registered as a common in 1965, and has been managed by a trust in recent years. Continue to follow the main path west, ie away from the road, ignoring smaller turnings to left and right, and eventually past another seat, to bear right past a tall hedge to a gate.

4 Go through the gate to head north, towards the sea, along a broad grassy path between some hedges, known as Green Common

Lane. As you go gently downhill, you will enjoy magnificent views of the coastline. When the track reaches a T-junction, turn left to head west, ignoring the turning to the right.

5 The track then bends right to continue north to the main coast road. This point is roughly your

The site of Branodunum Roman Fort

Brancaster is the Roman fort known as "Branodunum". Being quite remote, it would have been a minor outpost, built in the second century AD, and established to guard against attack by sea.

half-way mark. Continue along this broad straight path, possibly of Roman origins, until you reach the main coast road (A149). Here, cross over, and go through a narrow gap in the hedge, and then through a kissing gate, into a meadow, where livestock may be grazing. This field is part of the Roman fort of Branodunum, and you should head for the information board

Barrow Common dates from at least the mid 18th century, and was requisitioned for military use during the Second World War

The Creek

in front of you to get more insight. The lack of any apparent stonework may be a little disappointing, but the stone was taken in medieval times to build Brancaster Church!

6 Follow the path around the edge of the fort to get to the north-west corner ie diagonally oppo-site to where you came in. Go through the kissing gate, cross the track, through another kissing gate, being careful of the nettles, and head north across the next field, still part of the fort, to go through a further kissing gate. You have now travelled 2 miles.

7 Here you turn right onto the coast path to head east. The reeded area to your left was the old Roman beach, where boats would

come ashore to the fort. This "beach" is now some way from the sea, as sand and mud have washed along the shore from the east, as part of a process known as longshore drift. To the north-west is the Royal West Norfolk Golf Club. Founded in 1892 it is now renowned as one of the world's top 100 golf courses. It is certainly remote, sandwiched as it is on a narrow strip of land between the salt-marshes and the sea, and often cut off at high tide. You will soon be on a wooden path, heading east, with the staithe straight ahead. Continue along this path for about half a mile, contin-uing your direction after the clearing. There may be cut reeds stacked to the left of the path. These will eventually used for thatching, as Norfolk reed is often considered the finest thatching

Royal West Norfolk Golf Club, founded in 1892, is known as one of the world's top golf courses. Remote, sandwiched on a narrow strip of land between the saltmarshes and the sea, it is often cut off at high tide.

material in the world. Go through a kissing gate, and continue east to the green.

8 Turn left to follow a short path to the left of a row of houses. Then follow the path round as it leads you back to the staithe.

3 Wells-next-the-Sea

Quay, Coast Path and town: Boats, meadows and shops

The town of Wells-next-the-sea is now about a mile from the open sea itself, but in Tudor times, when it enjoyed much easier access to the sea, it was one of the great ports of eastern England, trading mainly in corn. This trade continued until relatively recently, with the Granary and its iconic loading gantry built in 1903. It is still the only commercially viable port on the North Norfolk Coast, but nowadays it is mainly fish that are landed here. The walk takes you along the quay, through a small maritime industrial estate, and along a section of the embankment forming

Start/Parking: Stearman's Yard car park, Freeman Street, Wells. Local Council charges.
Map Ref: TF 914438
Nearest postcode: NR23 1BH
Distance: 3.3 miles
Refreshments: Cafes and pubs in town centre.
Toilets: Public toilets on car park.
Terrain: Pavements and level paths along bank and through meadow. Short climb and descent.
Transport: Coasthopper bus
Pushchairs: NO
Difficulty: 🥾 🥾

the coastal path. You will return through a meadow, along a short section of disused railway trackbed, and back through the town centre. It is possible to cut short the walk should you wish.

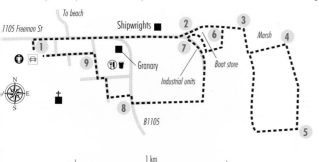

To beach

1105 Freeman St

Shipwrights ■

Granary

Boat store

Industrial units

Marsh

B1105

1 km
approximate scale

Boats and sky, Wells-next-the-Sea

1. From the car park, head north onto Freeman Street, and turn right to head east towards the quay. Ignore Beach Road, but continue east along the quayside, pausing to watch the boats if you wish. You will pass the century-old Dutch clipper *Albatros*, which was the last sail trader in and out of the UK, carried its last cargo in 1996, and now operates as a bar, based semi-permanently in Wells. During her chequered history, she has carried Jews to safety, used disaffected youngsters as

part of her crew and played a major part in a Greenpeace education project. Continue east, past the landmark granary loading gantry, and the chandlers. The road then takes you past the Shipwrights, a traditional Wells pub which closed in the 1990's and is now in private ownership. Continue east past the houses, the ingenious slipway trol-

ley, and Wells Sailing Club, then fork left at some marine industrial units.

2. Continue east along the grassy path to the left of the boat store, and you will soon leave behind the developed area, and be walking along the raised embankment which serves as the sea defence, but also

Beach essentials for sale

In Tudor times Wells-next-the-sea was one of the great ports of eastern England, trading mainly in corn. This trade continued until relatively recently, with the Granary and its iconic loading gantry built in 1903.

doubles as part of the North Norfolk Coastal Path, a long distance footpath that runs for 46 miles from Hunstanton to Cromer. You will have superb views over the marshes along here, but the walk can be a bracing one if the wind is from the east!

 After a while the path bends to the right, and you will have

covered 1 mile. At this point the path used to continue east down the bank and across the marsh, crossing the creek by means of a wooden footbridge. However this has now decayed, and you will need to follow the embankment round to the right then soon to the left, to continue heading east. *(If ever the footbridge gets reinstated, take*

this route, then turn right to rejoin the path at the end of the marsh).

When you reach the next corner, with bushes and small trees, turn right, and go down the slope into a meadow. Follow the path along the left edge of this meadow, until you pass some bushes on your right. Then you will fork right to follow

The Granary and Quay

The meadow

the path through the grass, heading broadly south-east.

5 As soon as the track has crossed the stream, (which might be dried up), turn sharp right to head west, with a small creek to your right. (Had you not turned right, your path would take you to the main coast road to the east of Wells). You will see the church tower in the distance, and you should head towards this. Follow the path as it bends right at the end of the field, which may not be clear if the grass is tall, then climb back on to the coast path to retrace your steps for a

short distance. You will have covered 1.5 miles. At the corner turn left to continue west along the path you came out along.

6 When the bath bends slightly to the right, branch left to leave the path and go back down the slope to a track heading south. This track soon bends right, and you will be heading west again, with allotments

Marshes and Creek

Sailing boats

on your left. When the houses start, there will be a track off to your right, just before a disused railway bridge and the start of the tarmac. This track will take you back down to the boat store, and you will turn left to briefly rejoin the coast path.

7 When you reach the tarmac turn left along the track past the crabbing sheds, with piles of crab pots outside. You will now be on the trackbed of a short stretch of railway which led from the town's main railway station down to the harbour, but the

tracks have long since been removed. Continue south under the bridge and at the end of the path turn right to head towards the church tower again. You have now covered 2.5 miles. The road takes you past a sales yard for caravans, and you will soon emerge at a bookshop which was Wells railway station until the early 1960's. The railway arrived in Wells in 1857 from Fakenham, (with the harbour branch opening in 1859), and continued on to the west as a light railway along what must have been a very scenic route through Holkham to Heacham, on the Hunstanton to Kings Lynn line in 1866. The great floods of 1953 caused extensive damage to the track, which was never repaired, so the continuing freight services terminated at Burnham Market. Train services to Wells finished completely in 1964.

8 Turn right along the B1105 for a short way, then left along an alleyway, or "loke", called School Alley, beside the old school, which is now Wells Field Study Centre, operated by Norfolk County Council. At the end of this path, turn right into the High Street, then left at the end into Station Road, then almost immediately right into Staithe Street, which is the main shopping street for Wells.

9 After a while, turn left into the narrow Anchor Lane, which is easily missed, and continue your direction west past the Methodist Church. Then turn right into Lugger Lane and back into the top of the car park where you started.

Railway trackbed

The railway arrived in Wells in 1857 from Fakenham, with the harbour branch opening in 1859, and continued on to the west as a light railway along what must have been a very scenic route through Holkham to Heacham

4 Blakeney

Quay and Fresh Marshes: Boats, marshes and open skies

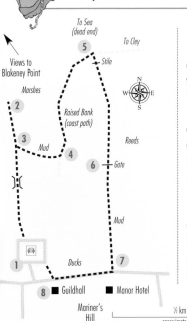

To Sea (dead end)

To Cley

5

Stile

Views to Blakeney Point

Marshes

2

Raised Bank (coast path)

Reeds

3

Mud

4

6

Gate

Mud

1

Ducks

7

8 ■ Guildhall   ■ Manor Hotel

Mariner's Hill

½ km
approximate scale

Blakeney is now a popular coastal village with yachtsmen, walkers, and summer holidaymakers, yet it was once a thriving port. It was the last working port on the Glaven Estuary, only falling into disuse in the early years of the 20th century. The quay, with its impressive view of the marsh, is approached by narrow roads, lined with flint cottages, that run down from the coast road.

This is a short but bracing walk across the marshes adjacent to Blakeney quay and channel. A splendid walk in dry weather, the track can be rather muddy in winter, so decent

Start/Parking: Blakeney Quay car park – Free to National Trust members.
Map Ref: TG 028442
Nearest postcode: NR25 7ND
Distance: 1.5 miles
Refreshments: Blakeney Quay – Teas and ice creams. Pubs and hotels in village.
Toilets: Blakeney Quay
Terrain: Flat – one short descent from the bank. Muddy in places.
Transport: Coasthopper bus
Pushchairs: NO
Difficulty: 🥾🥾

boots are recommended. If you are lucky you may see a flock of geese flying over.

Head north from the car park alongside the creek, ie away from the village. This path is well used in the summer, but can be a little muddy in winter, and may not be passable if there is a very high tide. Continue your direction over a wooden bridge, and follow a line of posts to an area of shingle after a big white post.

Soon the path ends, but pause to admire the view before turning round. On the horizon almost

The Creek

straight ahead is the Watch House, or "Half Way House" as it is often called – Built in 1865 as a coastguard house, sold to the Girl Guides Association in 1932, and now used as holiday accommodation. To the left of the Watch House, ie North West, is Blakeney Point, with the Pinewoods of Wells beyond that in the distance. The picturesque Cley Mill is to your right. At this point, turn round and head back south towards the village, this time taking the path a few feet to the left (ie East) of the path you came out along.

Turn left about 100 yards after the big white post to cut across to the raised bank, taking care to avoid any mud. *(If you wish, you can, of course, turn right along this bank to head back toward the car park.)*

Turn left on the bank to head North. You will be surrounded by marshes, but the path itself is usually quite busy. After a while you will pass a wrecked boat on your left.

When the path bends to the right, you will have walked about 0.9 miles, and you will have three options: The path to your left heads towards the sea, but is a dead end, so you would have to double back in due course. You could continue on the main path for another two miles to reach the village of Cley, but to return to your car you will have a further mile

Shrubby sea blight

which can be very wet in winter.

The path may not be clear, but head south toward the left-hand side of the solitary bush on the far side of the meadow. Then go past a patch of water on your right, and head for the gate.

6. Go over a stile, then continue south along the track with reeds either side. The track crosses a stream, and is muddy in places. This area is Blakeney Freshes. Continue along the track to the end, where it emerges across the road from the Manor Hotel.

of main road to cover. To continue with this walk however, turn right, go down the bank to a stile, which you climb over and head across the meadow,

Blakeney was the last working port on the Glaven Estuary, only falling into disuse in the early years of the 20th century

(7) At this point, you could explore the patch of National Trust land along the road to your left, or simply turn right, and back along the road to the car park. You will pass an enclosure containing a very comprehensive collection of birds looked after by the Blakeney Wildfowlers Association, which are worth pausing to look at.

(8) Do visit the Medieval Guildhall before returning to your car. This is the remains of the house of a

The Freshes

prosperous Blakeney merchant, with a fine 15th-century brickvaulted undercroft. Later it was the Guildhall of Blakeney's guild of fish merchants. Finally, if you are feeling energetic, why not climb the adjoining Mariners Hill, built originally as a harbour lookout or beacon mount. The harbour views are well worth it, and there is no finer spot to enjoy your picnic!

Medieval Guildhall

The Watch House, or "Half Way House" as it is often called. Built in 1865 as a coastguard house, sold to the Girl Guides association in 1932, and now used as holiday accommodation

5 **Cley**

Nature Reserve and beach: Shingle, sea and marsh

A bracing walk along the shingle bank forming part of the stunning North Norfolk coastal path. You have the option of going into the reserve itself, but the Norfolk Wildlife Trust make a charge for this. There is no charge to park at or to visit the fabulous new eco-friendly visitor centre, with excellent views across the marshes. A wide variety of birds inhabit these marshes, but watch out in particular for the reclusive Bittern, Redshanks, and Marsh Harriers.

The Government's "Managed Retreat" policy has allowed the shingle bank, which for many years protected the villages of Salthouse and Cley to controversially collapse, allowing the sea to invade at time, the marshes threatening both wildlife and people's homes.

Start/Parking: Norfolk Wildlife Trust Visitor Centre Car Park – Free – adjacent to Coast Road.
Map Ref: TG 054441
Nearest postcode: NR25 7SA
Distance: 3 miles
Refreshments: NWT visitor centre
Toilets: NWT visitor centre
Terrain: Good paths, shingle. Mainly flat –one short descent.
Transport: Coasthopper bus
Pushchairs: NO
Difficulty:

From the visitor centre, take the path north leading down to the reserve. Carefully cross the busy Coast Road (A149) and immediately turn right into a grassy path between a small river and the main road. Continue east along this grassy path, which may be a little damp in places in winter, until you reach a small car park.

Climb onto the bank beside the car park, and head north toward the sea (away from the road). You will enjoy uninterrupted views across the marshes, with possibly cattle to your right, and reed-beds to the left, where birds are often to be seen. After about half a mile you will reach Arnolds Marsh on your right (owned by the National Trust), then more water on your left.

Visit the new eco-friendly visitor centre, with excellent views across the marshes. A wide variety of birds inhabit these marshes, but watch out in particular for the reclusive Bittern, Redshanks, and Marsh Harriers.

National Wetlands Trust Reserve

The footpath to Cley

(3) When you reach what is left of the shingle bank, climb onto the bank and admire the views. You can see the hills of Sheringham to your right, and should be just able to make out the lifeboat house on the beach. Turn left to head West. The area to your left is Cley Eye, and you will see Cley Windmill, also on your left in the distance, as well as Blakeney Church on the higher ground. Proceed west for about 0.75 miles.

(4) You will eventually reach the beach car park, by which time you will have walked about 1.5 miles. If you are feeling energetic, a further 4 miles west along the shingle bank will take you to Blakeney Point, but don't forget it's another 4 miles return, with no other way back !

From the car park, the road heads inland. Climb onto the grassy bank and take the path heading south which runs beside the road. Cley Mill will now be ahead of you, and there may be cows to your left. Follow this path all the way to the village of Cley, past a round iron structure, almost certainly a wartime pill box.

Iron pill box

Cley marshes

 5 If you are agile, you could turn left just before the iron structure, scramble down the bank, and cross the bridge to bring you out on Beach Road. Otherwise proceed a little further along the path where the descent to Beach Road may be a bit easier.

You have the option instead of continuing along the path into the middle of the village, but you will need to return to Beach Road afterwards.

6 From Beach Road, turn left onto a new gravel path

heading east, parallel to the Coast Road. Shortly this meets a boardwalk. At this point, turning left would take you onto the reserve (for which there is a charge), right would take you onto the main road. However, continue straight on along the boardwalk, which bends left, over a bridge, then right, to take you back to the visitor centre, and a well-earned cup of tea.

Coastal erosion

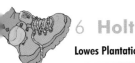

6

Holt

6 Holt

Lowes Plantation: Woodland, heath and bog

H olt Lowes is a remnant of the great belt of heathland that was found in North Norfolk between Cromer and Holt, extending south all the way to Norwich. This heathland had been formed on the deposits of sands and gravels that had been dumped by the retreating glaciers of various Ice Ages. But the vegetation itself is the result of man's activities since the Bronze Age, ie grazing, burning and periodic cultivation. In the 19th and 20th centuries much of this heathland has been ploughed up and reclaimed for agriculture, or planted with coniferous trees, the remainder allocated as commons or 'poors' allotments, being regarded as poor agricultural land. More recently, the town of Holt had a miraculous escape when, in a thunderstorm on 19 August 1968, a Victor B2 plane from RAF Marham collided with a Canberra, showering flaming debris over a large area of the plantation, killing both crews, a total of 7 men. The Lowes is now a Site of Special Scientific Interest and a Special Area of Conservation on account of the outstanding wildlife to be found there.

A148 to Cromer

Hempstead Road

2 Mud / Slope

3 Gate

4 Bog / Gorse

Holt Country Park

8 Stile

5

Holt Lowes

Clearing

Viewing Tower

Trees

7

6

Trees / Heather

1 km approximate scale

Start/Parking: Small car park just off the Hempstead Road from Holt – Free – Turn right just past cash & carry warehouse.
Map Ref: TG 088382
Nearest postcode: NR25 6EE
Distance: 1.5 miles
Refreshments: Holt town centre (0.6 miles)
Toilets: Holt Country Park (main car park, off Norwich Road)
Terrain: Woodland paths – some mud. Mainly flat, some gentle slopes.
Transport: None
Pushchairs: With difficulty
Difficulty:

33

Silver Birch

1 Leave the car park, heading directly away from the road, with the warehouse on your right.

Bear left then right, (ignoring the path straight ahead which would take you back to the road).

2 Cross the mud, then head up the slope, fork left, and continue to a 5 bar gate.

3 Go through the 5-bar gate, then go straight on to the Lowes Plantation, taking the smaller lower path to the left through the trees. (Ignore the main path to the right, which is your return route). Follow a twisty but clear path between gorse bushes and bracken. As you bear round to the right, the soft rush growing to your left is evidence of the boggy ground there.

The town of Holt had a miraculous escape when, in a thunderstorm on 19 August 1968, a Victor B2 plane from RAF Marham collided with a Canberra, showering flaming debris over the plantation, killing a total of 7 men.

4 Cross a muddy patch, then soon keep to the path on the left through the trees. The path shortly curves to the right, with the Glaven valley on the left (although you cannot see the river from here). More bogland is evident, this time supporting reeds. These are the kind of reeds which appear in much bigger quantities around the Norfolk Broads, and are used for thatching.

5 Continue your direction ignoring paths going off to the right. You will pass a rhododendron bush on the left, and the path is quite distinct here. Eventually the path broadens, and you should continue your direction south to a clearing. This area will normally be covered in gorse, but this had been cleared when I visited, probably to encourage more heathland wildlife.

Ignore the track to your right, but fork left and continue your direction, with bogland still on your left, and views over the Glaven valley.

6 Continue on this path until you are well past the next group of trees, when the path will curve to the right, and proceed across the heath,

where the ground is covered in flints and heather. The path goes through a clump of trees, and unfortunately you can sometimes hear the traffic noise from the Norwich road, but your path eventually curves right to head toward the pine tree-tops of the country park. A viewing platform will come into view in the trees, and you should head for this.

Bracket fungus

7 When you reach the 5-bar gate, turn right to head back towards the car park. You will have travelled one mile by now. *You may deviate left if you wish, to get to a pond with seats, but you must return to the 5 bar gate. Alternatively, you may go through the gate, and climb the viewing tower, which affords fine views over the plantation. (If you do this, go back through the gate afterwards, and turn left to*

Flints on the heath

head back in the direction of the car park.) You will now be heading North-East, following the fence along the edge of the country park, avoiding the mud where necessary. Baconsthorpe water tower may be visible on the horizon to your right. After a short while, watch out for a stile made from two carved statues, jolly fellows having a tug-of-war.

8 At this point, you can EITHER, go over the stile and continue to the T-junction, where you turn right, and continue to the end of the path, ignoring all left turns, OR continue your direction until you get to the 5-bar gate you encountered near the start of the walk, then turn left. Either way, you will be back on the path you came out along, and you should re-trace your steps to the car park.

Viewing tower

Holt Lowes is a remnant of the great belt of heathland that was found in North Norfolk between Cromer and Holt, extending south all the way to Norwich. This heathland had been formed on the deposits of sands and gravels that had been dumped by the retreating glaciers of various Ice Ages.

7 Kelling

Muckleburgh Hill: Heath, hilltop and sea views

Start/Parking: By roadside in Weynor
Gardens, off the coast road, to west of Weybourne.
Map Ref: TG 103428
Nearest postcode: NR25 7EQ
Distance: 0.8 miles
Refreshments: Weybourne Maltings Hotel,
Weybourne Ship PH, Kelling Pheasant Hotel.
Toilets: Pubs and hotels as above (for
customers).
Terrain: Woodland path, long gentle climb
and reasonably steep descent.
Transport: Coasthopper bus
Pushchairs: NO
Difficulty: 🥾 🥾 🥾

A short walk which includes a climb
up Muckleburgh Hill, with wonderful
views over the sea, with Blakeney Point
in the distance, the village of
Weybourne, and the old RAF station. In
Roman times, this was the site of one
of a chain of beacons, lit to summon
help in case of invasion. The stretch of
coast, known as Weybourne Hope, has
been recognized ever since as a likely
invasion target, because of the steeply
sloping beach which would enable
boats to draw close to the shore, hence
the age-old couplet: "He who old
England would hope to win, Must at
Weybourne Hope begin". Weybourne
camp was established nearby in 1936

and was used for coastal defence during the Second World War, but closed
in 1958. 30 years later a military
museum, the nationally renowned
Muckleburgh Collection opened to the
east of the current radar station.

NORTH SEA

Kelling Hard   ▬ Reserve Radar Station

6

Airstrip

5   7

Views

N
W E
S

Fox Hill   Muckleburgh
Hill

4

Gate

Gate

Gate

Gate

2

Weynor
Gardens

1

A149 Coast Road   Gates   To Weybourne

¼ km
approximate scale

Information sign

3 At this point you turn right through the gate and start the gentle uphill climb. *(You do have the option of following the fence, which would take you around the foot of the hill to the north, instead of climbing the hill, so you would miss the best views.)*

4 Bear right to climb the hill in front of you, known as Fox Hill, then continue straight on to the next hill, which is Muckleburgh Hill. You will have covered half a mile from the start of the walk.

1 Return to the main Coast Road (A149). Cross the road and go through the kissing gate onto the heathland the other side. Turn left through another gate, then immediately right to follow a fence heading north-west.

2 After a while there will be another kissing gate in the fence, and later a 5-bar gate, but you ignore both these. By now the scenery will have become more open, and you will soon find another gate in the fence.

Above: tree – Above right: Woody path

(5) At the top of this hill you will have excellent views of the surrounding countryside — the Muckleburgh collection, Weybourne village, the Pheasant Hotel, and the MoD radar station at Kelling, as well as over the sea itself. You might even be lucky enough to see a private plane take off or land on the small grassy airstrip. Standing up here, it is easy to understand the strategic importance of this area in defending the coast.

There is only one other path down the hill, which is almost due North (towards the sea). Take this path, through the bracken if in late summer, continuing your direction until you get to the bottom. *(You could, if you preferred, turn right half-way down, along a steeper stony path, then turn left to emerge further down the main path.)*

6 Turn right at the T-junction and keep going (heading east).

7 When you reach the clearing, ignore the turning to the right, but continue down the hill to get back to the main road. Cross the road and return to Weynor Gardens.

Radar station

Muckleburgh Hill, in Roman times, was the site of one of a chain of beacons, lit to summon help in case of invasion. The stretch of coast, known as Weybourne Hope, has been recognized ever since as a likely invasion target, because of the steeply sloping beach which would enable boats to draw close to the shore, hence the age-old couplet: 'He who old England would hope to win, Must at Weybourne Hope begin'. Weybourne camp was established in 1936 for Anti-Aircraft Training, and the Royal Norfolk Regiment were stationed here on coastal defence duty during World War II.

8 Weybourne

Kelling Heath and Railway Path: Heath and steam trains

The first section of this walk runs along-side the North Norfolk Railway, known as "The Poppy Line", heading from Weybourne towards Holt. This line used to be part of the M&GN line from Cromer to the Midlands, closed by Dr Beeching in April 1964. The North Norfolk Railway re-opened the section from Sheringham to Weybourne in 1976, and extended the line up the hill through Kelling Heath to High Kelling in 1989, where it was pre-vented from getting any further by the Holt bypass which had been built on the old M&GN trackbed.

The walk continues across Kelling Heath itself. The heath runs to some 250 acres, and as well as the caravan site also hosts a wildlife reserve with nature trails, and a Red Squirrel breed-ing program. It is possible to view a small compound where the red squirrels are housed, but

Start/Parking: Small stony Car Park just over the railway bridge to the south of Weybourne Station- free.
Map Ref: TG 118419
Nearest postcode: NR25 7HN
Distance: 2.3 miles
Refreshments: Weybourne Railway Station, Kelling Heath Campsite (both when open).
Toilets: Weybourne Railway Station
Terrain: Mainly level heathland paths, with one steep climb, and one gentle descent.
Transport: North Norfolk Railway (the Poppy Line)
Pushchairs: NO
Difficulty: 🥾 🥾

they are timid and not always visible. You may be lucky enough to spot the rare Silver Studded Blue butterfly some of which were released on the heath in 2001 after they had become extinct in the 1970s, and are now multiplying.

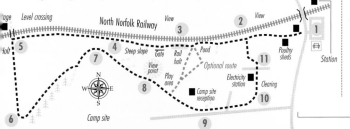

Woodland path

2 A little further on some "view-ing poles" have been set up, which do nothing to enhance your view, but which direct your gaze to specific landmarks described on the information boards. But there is a seat here if you need a rest. Continue your direction past a lily-covered pond, ignoring a path to the left. The main path then continues uphill toward the caravan site, but you should turn right here, taking a smaller path which leads to the railway halt. The track

1 Leave the car park, and cross the road. Head west along a public footpath past a telephone pole, following a neat path with a bungalow to your right. Go straight on into a narrow path with chicken sheds to your left. Follow the path through the woods, and you will find a pond below you on the right. Shortly after this, the path meets the railway line, and there will be views over Weybourne towards the sea on your right.

Pond

gradient is quite steep (for a railway), and steam trains will not stop here on the way UP the hill, as the locomotives find it difficult to start again without wheelspin. Passengers wishing to board or leave the train here must do so on the downhill journey! You will have covered half a mile at this point.

(3) Cross the platform, and continue west following the path beside the railway track.

Kelling Heath runs to some 250 acres, and as well as the caravan site also hosts a wildlife reserve with nature trails, and a Red Squirrel breeding program.

Follow the path through the trees, never more than about 50 yards from the railway line, and go past a 5-bar gate. The straight grassy slope on your left used to be used as a ski slope, but there is rarely enough snow these days! Fork right at the foot of this

Bluebells

Steam train

slope to continue your direction west, with a short but steep climb to get back to the fence alongside the railway track, which will be below you on your right. Pause to admire the view to the East before continuing. The railway is at its steepest at this point, and if you are lucky to see a locomotive storming up this bank, it will be a marvellous display of power.

The old crossing

Gorse and conifers

(4) The path becomes sandy here, with much gorse in evidence. The wider path at the top of the hill acts as a firebreak, to avoid any sparks from the steam engines setting light to the heath.

Continue your direction west beside the railway until you get to a old unmanned crossing, with a small crossing-keeper's cottage. The crossing is rarely used these days, other than for foot traffic, and the cottage is a private home. Continuing along the path would eventually take you to the railway terminus at Holt. You have now travelled one mile.

(5) At this point you should turn left to leave the railway, and head south towards the caravan site.

Bridle path

You will be crossing heathland now, with some mud, and much heather and, of course, gorse.

(6) When you reach the pine trees, turn left just before the dog bin, to follow a bridleway, with a few pine trees to your right (most have been chopped down now) and the camp site beyond them. As you continue to head

east, a path joins from the right, but continue your direction, to be rewarded with sea glimpses as you progress.

(7) When you are almost back at the railway line, turn right at the butterfly waymark, and follow this path, ignoring the downhill paths to your left as you proceed. You have covered 1.5 miles.

(8) When you reach the viewing platform with information boards, pause a while to admire the views towards the sea. Then continue heading east past a flint cairn. If you wish to follow the nature trail across the heath, a brochure is available from the camp site reception. Continue past the caravans ignoring the "Heron 7 - 9" sign and bear right along the main

Viewpoint

Weybourne village

Silver Studded Blue
butterfly are multiplying
since their release on
the heath in 2001, after
they had become extinct
in the 1970s.

path toward the camp site's central complex, then take a path to the left, which brings you out at the shopping and reception area. Refreshments are available here in the season.

9 Cross the paved area, and head east along the main entrance road to the campsite. Ignore the path to the left signed "Bottom pond and North Norfolk railway" and ignore a wide path to the left soon after. Where possible take the path

through the trees to the left of the road, but parallel to it, and ignore a further grassy clearing on the left.

10 The next grassy clearing on the left is the one you should take, and it will lead you past a small electricity substation.

11 Cross the track and continue your direction down the grassy slope, turning left at the bottom to continue your downhill journey. This

will bring you out at the viewing poles you passed near the beginning of your walk. Turn right here and retrace your steps back to the car park.

Weybourne station

9 Sheringham

Skelding Hill and Beach: Beach and clifftops

A short but vigorous walk along the shingle beach west of Sheringham, returning along the cliff tops on the golf course, and over Skelding Hill, with its stunning views. The cliffs in this area are mainly sand, having been deposited by the melting glacier at the last ice age some 12,000 years ago. Consequently the cliffs are prone to erosion, with the rainwater draining from the land causing the cliffs to "slump", and the sea transporting the sand and shingle along the coast to form spits like Blakeney Point. Fortunately the higher beach along this stretch offers some protection to the cliff, and the rate of erosion is less than further round the coast (to the east). Sheringham Golf Club was formed in 1891 as a nine hole course, which was extended in 1898 to a full eighteen holes. Noted for its long par 4 holes it is a severe test of players' ability, especially when the wind blows!

Start/Parking: The Leas, Sheringham – free.
Map Ref: TG 155435
Nearest postcode: NR26 8LY
Distance: 1.8 miles
Refreshments: Sheringham Promenade (or ice creams by the arch in summer)
Toilets: Sheringham Promenade (under the arch)
Terrain: Pebble beach and hilly cliff top. One steep climb and descent.
Transport: Bittern line railway, Buses (First Eastern, Sanders and others)
Pushchairs: NO
Difficulty: 🥾 🥾 🥾

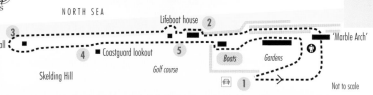

NORTH SEA

Lifeboat house

'Marble Arch'

Coastguard lookout

Boats   Gardens

Skelding Hill

Golf course

Not to scale

Lifeboat house

along the beach towards Weybourne. You will soon go past the tractor house (used to house the lifeboat tractor when Sheringham had an offshore boat which filled the boathouse), and then past the last groyne.

You will need to continue west along the stones for just over half a mile. You will soon get used to walking on the stones, although it is more hard work than level ground, and thick-soled shoes are advisable.

1 Head towards the sea down-hill under the arch opposite the approach road, (known locally as "Marble Arch"), then left down the slope to the promenade. Head west past the café to the lifeboat house, built in 1936 when the first motor lifeboat arrived in the town.

2 Go past the boathouse (or visit if you wish), then cross the concrete and down the slope onto the pebbles, and continue heading West

Sheringham beach

(3) After a while, the cliffs get lower to meet the beach, and there is a concrete outfall from the Splash swimming pool, which marks your halfway point. This is "The Hythe" where the fishermen used to launch their boats until the 19th century. The earliest settlement was also in this spot, but moved to the higher ground about 500 years ago to enjoy greater protection from the sea.

At this point you need to climb onto the cliff – you might find this easier by continuing for about 30m past the out-

Beach stones

fall. You could then turn right and continue west toward Weybourne (about two miles distant), but you would also need to return! Instead, turn left to head east back towards Sheringham. You are now on the coast path, which you will follow all the way back, keeping to the path and NOT straying onto the golf course. Also take care near the cliff edge. As you climb the first, small hill, you will see the North Norfolk Railway to your right (you might be lucky enough to see a steam train), and Skelding Hill ahead of you.

(4) When you have climbed Skelding Hill, which is steeper, pause at the top to admire the view, taking advantage of the seats provided. Blakeney Point may just be visible to the West, the trees of Sheringham Park

The cliffs in this area are mainly sand, having been deposited by the melting glacier at the last ice age some 12,000 years ago. Consequently the cliffs are prone to erosion, with the rainwater draining from the land causing the cliffs to "slump", and the sea transporting the sand and shingle along the coast to form spits like Blakeney Point.

Sheringham

to the South, and the town of Sheringham with Beeston Hump beyond to the East. You may just see the flashing light of Cromer lighthouse in the distance (to the East).

Also at the top of the hill is the local Coastwatch station, where volunteers keep a log of passing craft, and watch out for any potential emergencies on the cliffs or beach. This used to be the coastguard lookout, until the govern-

ment discontinued the use of such lookouts some years ago. Continue East as you descend the hill and head back into Sheringham.

(5) After a while the lifeboat house will be below you on your left, and you will continue east to emerge at the boating lake where there is a shelter and seats. From here it is a short walk back to your car.

View west from Skelding Hill

Sheringham Golf Club was formed in 1891 as a nine hole course, which was extended in 1898 to a full eighteen holes. Noted for its long par 4 holes it is a severe test of players' ability, especially when the wind blows!

10 West Runton

Incleborough Hill: Woodland, hilltop and sea views

This walk starts close to the village of West Runton, whose beach contains some superb rock pools. The sandy cliffs, deposits from the last ice age some 12,000 years ago, have been known to yield some interesting fossils. The most fascinating of these came to light after the storms in December 1990 when remains of a 11 ton steppe mammoth, a mammuthus trogontherii, supposedly 700,000 years old, were spotted by a walker on the beach. Not fully excavated until 1995, the West Runton Elephant is said to be the biggest, most complete and best preserved fossilized elephant skeleton ever found.

Start/Parking: On road where Renwick Park & Calves Well Lane meet Sandy Lane heading south from West Runton

Map Ref: TG 183421

Nearest postcode: NR27 9LT

Distance: 1.1 miles

Refreshments: Village Inn and Cafe in West Runton village. Links Hotel – Fairways Bar.

Toilets: Links Hotel (for customers)

Terrain: Countryside paths with a hill to climb and descend.

Transport: Railway – Bittern Line – West Runton Station

Pushchairs: NO – some steep sections.

Difficulty: 🐾 🐾 🐾

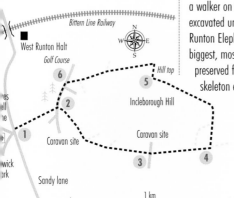

Bittern Line Railway

West Runton Halt

Golf Course

6

2

1

Caravan site

Sandy lane

Hill top

5

Incleborough Hill

Caravan site

3

4

es
ell
ne

wick
ark

1 km
approximate scale

Hilltop

1. From the junction of Renwick Park, Calves Well Lane and Sandy Lane, cross to the eastern side of the road, and head east along a track signposted "Restricted Byway", which goes past a few houses before getting narrower, and passing a number of back gardens. After a while, the path emerges onto a tarmac track which leads to the caravan club site.

Caravan site

2. You should turn left, then almost immediately right onto a path that goes alongside the caravan site, with the caravans to your right. You will start off heading south-east, but the path soon bends to the left so that you are heading east, gently climbing all the while. Ignore any paths to the left, which would simply take you onto the golf course. Your path will eventually descend quite sharply, still heading east, to meet another road through the caravan site.

3. Cross this road to continue east along the path marked "public footpath". Once you have gone through a kissing gate, you will have entered the National Trust area known as Incleborough Hill. Continue east

View to north-west

along the main path. After a while you will reach a junction with a clearly marked path to the left. You can turn left here, or along the next path a few yards further on.

(4) After a short climb you will soon reach a grassy hilltop with lovely views towards Cromer and the sea. You may wish to pause here

for a wander, a sit down on the seats provided, or even to consume a picnic! To continue the walk, turn left to head roughly west and follow the path which climbs to the top of the hill. You can see where the gorse has been cleared in order to open up the views, and to allow other plant life to grow. The views at the top are well worth the climb. As you face the sea, Cromer is to your right, West Runton to your left

with Sheringham beyond, and the coastline stretching west towards Blakeney beyond that.

(5) Continue the walk by heading briefly north towards the sea, then bend left to follow the path west towards West Runton church which will be clearly visible. Near the seat, you will spot a path to your right but this is steep and bumpy, so you should keep

Cromer

to the main path heading west. After going past the seat your path will start heading down the hill towards the golf course, but near the bottom of the hill, ignore the left turning which would take you back up the hill.

6 Almost immediately go through the kissing gate at the bottom, and turn left to head south west along the main path. You will soon reach a road leading into the caravan site. Cross straight over to head along the tarmac track alongside the pine trees which is a public track across the Links Country Park Golf Course. The track takes you back to the other entrance of the caravan site, which is where you turned off near the beginning of the walk. From here you should retrace your steps along the path to Renwick Park.

View to the west

The Links Country Park Golf Course was designed in 1903 by golf pioneer John Henry Taylor, who described it as "one of the most sporting golf courses in England." At that time the course was 18 holes, and 6125 yards long, but in 1940 was taken over by the War Office as a training area. Parts of the course were sold, so when the club re-opened in 1950 it had become a 9 hole course.

11 Cromer

Town, Beach and Cliffs: Seaside, shops and a lighthouse

An interesting walk with fine views over the sea and the town of Cromer. In Medieval times Cromer was called Shipden, and was half a mile north of the present cliffs! The ravages of the sea drove the settlement south to what is now Cromer, and the wealth generated by the wool trade, and in particular the ability to weave Worstead cloth, enabled the people of Cromer to build the prestigious church, completed in 1437. The arrival of the railways in Cromer in 1877, boosted Cromer's fortunes as a fashionable holiday resort, and triggered off major building works, resulting in much of the current town. The walk will take you along promenade and beach,

Start/Parking: Cromer – Runton Road Cliff Car Park on main road to west of Cromer. Council charges.

Map Ref: TG 212424
Nearest postcode: NR27 9AU

Distance: 3.5 miles (Less for shorter routes)

Refreshments: Numerous cafes, restaurants, pubs and ice cream stalls in the town.

Toilets: Toilets on the car park, promenade, pier and in the town.

Terrain: Paved paths, beach, long climb and descent. Optional long steep climb up steps.

Transport: First Eastern Counties & Sanders buses; Train – Bittern Line, Cromer station

Pushchairs: On shorter route only

Difficulty: 🐾 🐾 🐾
shorter route 🐾 🐾

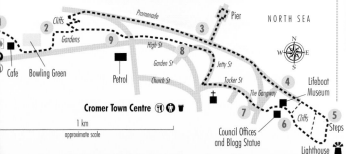

returning along a more elevated path on the cliffs, and through part of the town itself, with optional detours to visit attractions or sample local fare.

55

1 Park on the cliff top car park at Runton Road and take the path to the left of the wooden cafe near the toilets to emerge on the main road, where you turn left, then very soon left again to continue heading east, but with a hedge between you and the road. Cromer bowls club will be to your left. Continue along this path, but just before a few steps turn left to head north for a shelter and the cliff.

2 Turn right along the cliff path, with views of the pier, but very soon turn left onto a long but easy zig-zag path which leads down the cliff to the promenade (eventually!). (If you preferred you could descend by a long flight of white metal steps a little further on). At the bottom, turn right onto the promenade to continue heading

The promenade

east. As you proceed watch out for quotations from famous people which have been engraved on the ground.

3 When you reach the pier fore-court, you will see a number of lines radiating from a compass rose

The Pier from the cliff

showing the direction and date of historic Cromer Lifeboat rescues. By all means divert onto the pier and walk to the end, emulating the holidaymakers who have done the same over the century or more since the pier was built. The lifeboat station on the end of the pier houses the new state-of-the-art Tamar lifeboat, the Lester, carrying on the proud tradition of the Cromer station, whose most famous lifeboatman you will learn about later in your walk. You will have now covered about 0.75 miles. Return to the promenade, and turn left to continue heading east past the yellow Bath House. You will cross the Gangway, past a motley collection of fishing boats and their tractors, and past the new lifeboat museum, containing the famous *HF Bailey* lifeboat, responsible for saving many hundreds of lives. Feel free to stop off to visit the museum – there is no charge, and pause to enjoy refreshments in the excellent cafe over the museum.

The yellow Bath House, dating from 1814, is where Victorian visitors would enjoy hot and cold sea water baths in the basement! This later became a pub, but is now owned privately.

The Bath House

Cromer from the east

The arrival of the railways in Cromer in 1877, followed by a second station 10 years later, boosted Cromer's fortunes as a fashionable holiday resort, and triggered off major building works, resulting in much of the current town.

(4) Continue east along the promenade to the end of a row of brick beach huts. At this point you could turn right to climb up to the cliff path at the top, and if steps are a problem for you, then you should take this route. Otherwise continue east along the promenade, or along the beach. A little further on there are some wooden steps ascending the cliff between the beach huts, and you could take this route to the top. You have now walked 1.25 miles. For the full walk, however, continue to the end of the promenade and onto the beach, and continue east for a while, past the end of the low wooden sea wall, until you reach some steps going up the cliff before the next long groyne.

(5) The climb is long and steep, and when you reach the top

Beach huts

Cromer lighthouse will be directly ahead of you. This is Cromer's third lighthouse: The first was a beacon on Cromer church tower. The second sported a rotating oil light, but fell into the sea in 1866. The present lighthouse, 18m tall, was built in 1833, became electric-powered in 1958, and converted to automatic operation in June 1990, now monitored by Trinity House from Harwich. Go to get a closer look if you wish, but the walk continues by turning right to

Cromer Lighthouse

head west through Happy Valley and along the cliff top towards the town, enjoying views of the pier and sea as you do so.

You will soon go past the old coastguard lookout on your left, which was recently sold into private hands, and a little later you will go past houses on your left, with fine views on your right. As you go past the putting green, the path from the short route emerges onto the your path, and you continue west towards the town.

(6) You will soon go past the statue of the lifeboatman Henry Blogg. Continue along the path as it soon bends left then right to take you to the top of the Gangway. The full walk so far has been 2.8 miles. Note the flat strips of stone set into the cobbles to make it easier for the horses to pull the coal wagons up the steep slope, since Cromer's coal was unloaded from ships onto the beach until the railways arrived in the late 19th century. Note also the fact that the cobbles or "sets" are slightly angled, to help the horses hooves grip the road as they pulled the heavy loads.

(7) Cross the road, and turn right behind the metal railings. You will soon be heading west again, along East Cliff, and then along Tucker Street.

Henry Blogg is reputed to be the bravest, and one of the most modest, lifeboatmen who have ever lived. The inscription tells you about his tally of medals, and records the fact that, with his loyal crew, he saved 873 lives.

Cromer church

If you wish you can turn left along the path that leads to the town museum, and visit the museum, the town centre, or the church. The church tower is sometimes open to the public, and its 170 steps take you to the roof of the 50m tower, the tallest parish church in Norfolk, with stunning views over north Norfolk. Do admire the workmanship of the knapped flint in the walls of the church before heading back for the sea front. Turn Right down Jetty Street, beside Barclays Bank, enjoying a

flavour of Victorian Cromer, and emerge at the palatial Hotel de Paris on the cliff top, with views of the pier again.

(8) At this point you could divert into Garden Street for fish and chips. If not, continue west along the cliff, and take the main path beside the road when you reach the corner with Morrisons petrol station, to continue heading west along the cliff path.

Cromer from the pier

(9) You will go past some of the posh Victorian hotels which sprung up to accommodate the burgeoning holiday trade, and also past Albany Court flats which replaced the very Grand Hotel destroyed by fire in the 1960's. The cliff path leads back to the car park, but when you reach the shelter you may find the path diverted along the route you came out along, past the bowling green.

12 Overstrand

Tolls Hill and Village: Country paths and sea views

NORTH SEA

Sea Marge

Village

A149 Coast Road

Disused Railway

Tolls Hill

Madams
Lane

Northrepps

Wireless
Station

1 km
approximate scale

A pleasant walk which starts on the cliff top at Overstrand, just east of Cromer, and heads inland to Northrepps past the old railway station, then returns along a track back into the village to finish back at the cliffs. The fishing village of Overstrand was made famous by Clement Scott, a Daily Telegraph and Morning Post writer, who named the area Poppyland, because of the many wild red poppies which grew in the fields and on the cliffs. His romantic tales about the area drew the rich and famous, and Overstrand became

Start/Parking: Overstrand - sea front cliff top car park (Local Council charges)
Map Ref: TG 247411
Nearest postcode: NR27 0PF
Distance: 2.1 miles
Refreshments: Cliff top Cafe, just to the east of the car park
Toilets: Public toilets in the car park
Terrain: Pavements, tracks and country paths
Transport: Sanders coach services from Cromer
Pushchairs: With difficulty – some mud and gradients
Difficulty:

known as the Village of Millionaires, as can be seen from the many fine and interesting houses here.

Leaving the car park turn right to head west along the road leading away from the sea, ignoring two left turns. Turn left into a public footpath just after a telegraph pole. This brings you out onto the main coast road, which you should cross, and continue your direction south along the wide shingle path marked "footpath to Northrepps".

 This soon becomes a smaller grassy path which takes you

Maritime legacy

Old railway station

past some poultry sheds, still heading south. You will go past Overstrand's old railway station, which is now a private dwelling. The trackbed to the left is very overgrown, but the station building, platform and walkways are still clearly visible on the right. You will also go past some allotments on your left. You have now travelled half a mile.

 Fork right to continue on the way-marked path, stooping if necessary to clear the low bushes as

The railway line from Cromer High station to Mundelsey was established in 1898, but fell victim to the Beeching cuts in 1964.

the path climbs. You will then follow a clear path across a field, with the village of Northrepps visible in front of you. This is Tolls Hill, which is one of 250 County Wildlife sites in Norfolk. Continue south along the path between hedges until you reach the first houses, and the path becomes surfaced.

 When you reach the junction, which is 1 mile from your starting point, turn left into Madams Lane, to head north-east towards the wireless masts along a gently climbing path. When you reach the wireless station the path becomes surfaced, and you will have lovely views of the sea to the north, with Cromer lighthouse to your left. This VHF transmitter station was built in 1947 to provide communications between the Trimingham radar station a few miles to the east, and aircraft. It was closed when RAF Neatishead took over radar cover in 1963, and subsequently taken over by "National Air Traffic Services", part of

Wireless station

the Civil Aviation Authority. The path continues north, and soon reaches a bridge over the disused railway line, 1.5 miles into your walk.

5 The track then bends left then right to continue downhill towards Overstrand. When you reach the main road, cross over, and continue north down Carr Lane. Turn left at the bottom to go past the grade II listed Sea Marge on your right, an elegant

Sea Marge was the country home for Sir Edgar Speyer, a London banker, who was chairman and founder of London Underground. During the First World War, his German parentage and friendship with the Kaiser gave rise to many rumours including speculation that the Sea Marge was being used as a signaling point for German submarines! Sir Edgar was subsequently stripped of his knighthood and British nationality, and deported.

Edwardian mansion built in 1908. Between 1935 and 1955, Sea Marge was a hotel with Winston Churchill

'Stop me and buy one'

included in the guest list. After a spell as a nursing home, it reopened as a hotel and restaurant in 1996.

6 Go past the old village pump on your left, then turn right just after the White Horse pub and follow the road north to the cliff passing an unusual-looking Methodist chapel on your left, which was designed by Edwin Lutyens, the famous architect. After an optional stop at the "Cliff Top Café", head west along the cliff top, past the fishing boats and crab pots,

and then past a fine "Arts and Crafts" house called "The Pleasaunce", just visible over the flint wall to your left. Built in 1897-9, the Pleasaunce was developed by Lord and Lady Battersea with the help of the young Edwin Lutyens, who was just starting his architectural career. Architect and client apparently enjoyed a stormy relationship, with Lady Battersea reputedly throwing bricks from the balcony wall outside her bedroom until she considered it the correct height! The building is now a Christian guest house. Continue west for a few more yards, back to the car park.

Chapel designed by Sir Edwin Lutyens